The First Book of FRUITS

The First Book of
FRUITS

by Barbara L. Beck
pictures by Page Cary

FRANKLIN WATTS, INC.
575 Lexington Avenue • New York, N.Y. 10022

Library of Congress Catalog Card Number: 67-10225
© Copyright 1967 by Franklin Watts, Inc.
Printed in the United States of America
by Polygraphic Company of America

1 2 3 4 5

CONTENTS

The First Book of FRUITS

WHAT IS A FRUIT?

THE WORD "fruit" has two meanings. It all depends on who is talking. A botanist, or plant scientist, thinks of fruits in one way. To him, a fruit is the part of a growing plant that develops from a flower after it has withered. Usually this fruit holds seeds of some kind. It is a seed container. Some seed containers may be fruits we eat; some may not. To a botanist, the seedpods of lupine and of alfalfa are fruits. So are acorns and pea pods and milkweed pods and apples and walnuts and ears of corn, and all the hundreds and hundreds of other kinds of seed containers that flowering plants have.

Most people who are not plant scientists think of fruits in another way. To these people, fruits are the edible, good-tasting, fleshy plant products of certain trees or vines or bushes — the products we often buy in fruit stores. This book is about this latter kind of fruit.

HOW SEEDS ARE FORMED

A GREAT NUMBER of the land plants of the world grow from seeds.

The seeds develop within a flower. Usually the flower is made up of four parts. Many green, leaflike sepals make up the *calyx* — the cuplike part that covers the unopened flower bud and later holds the petals. Within the calyx is the *corolla*, which we usually see as the brightly colored petals of a flower. Inside the calyx and corolla are the male and female parts of the flower. The female parts are called *pistils*; the male parts are called *stamens*. Both the pistils and the stamens must play a part in forming seeds. Seed plants must have male and female parents, just as most animals must.

The male parts, the stamens, have slender stalks called *filaments*. At their ends are larger, boxlike growths called *anthers*. The anthers produce a fine dust called *pollen*, which is usually yellow.

The pistils also have stalks. These are called *styles*. At the top of each style is a part called the *stigma*; at the bottom is a hollow chamber called the *ovary*.

1

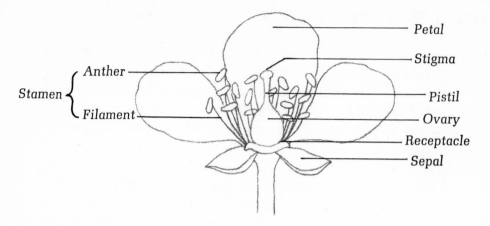

The parts of a flower. The sepals, all together, form the calyx. The petals, all together, form the corolla.

For seeds to form, pollen must be carried from the stamens of the flowers to the pistils. Sometimes pollen sticks to bees, moths, and other insects and they take it with them as they travel from one flower to another. Sometimes pollen is carried by the wind, the rain, or by hummingbirds who visit the flowers in search of nectar.

When a grain of pollen reaches the stigma of a pistil, it forms a tube that grows down the style into the ovary. Once in the ovary, the pollen joins with one of a number of eggs that have formed there, and a seed begins to grow.

When the seeds are formed, the wall of the ovary — and sometimes other parts of the flower — grows larger, surrounds the seeds, and finally becomes the fruit.

Not all flowers have both male and female parts. In some plants the stamens — the male parts — may be within one flower, while the pistils — the female parts — may be within another flower on the same plant, or on a nearby plant, or even within a blossom growing on a plant miles away.

Even when stamens and pistils grow within the same blossoms, some plants need the pollen of a flower from another plant in order to produce really good fruit.

2

SOME GROUPS OF FRUITS

THE PLANT products we ordinarily think of as fruits can be divided into several groups, depending on how their seed containers are formed. We can usually tell the groups apart by their appearance, although sometimes we find some surprises.

Drupe fruits usually contain a single seed enclosed in a hard, bony stone. Peaches, apricots, and cherries belong in this group.

Pome fruits have no stone, but have several seeds. These seeds are usually found within a papery central chamber. Apples and pears are pome fruits.

Berries are pulpy fruits that sometimes have many seeds, but not always. Dates are one-seed berries, and bananas are berries with no seeds. Grapes, blueberries, currants, and cranberries are berries. So are tomatoes.

Strawberries, raspberries, blackberries, and their like are not really berries, in spite of their names. They are *aggregate* fruits. A single aggregate fruit is made up of many tinier fruitlets, all clustered around one receptacle.

Multiple fruits come from the joined seed receptacles of several flowers. Figs, mulberries, and pineapples are multiple fruits.

Types of fruits

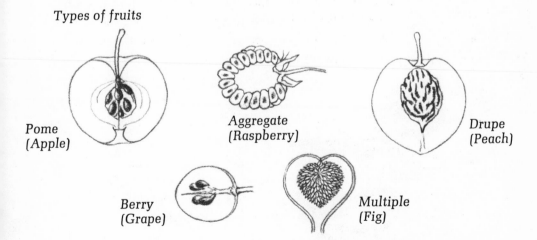

Pome
(Apple)

Aggregate
(Raspberry)

Drupe
(Peach)

Berry
(Grape)

Multiple
(Fig)

OTHER WAYS OF GROWING NEW PLANTS

NEW PLANTS may be formed in other ways besides seeding.

New raspberry plants, for instance, are grown by *layering*. A gardener bends a raspberry shoot to the ground and covers it with soil. After a while the part beneath the soil sends out roots — the beginning of a new plant.

New date trees are grown from suckers that come up around the base of the parent plant. These are cut off and put in the ground to grow.

In *budding* or *grafting*, buds or small twigs are cut from the parent tree and are attached to another seedling. This seedling may have poor fruit of its own, but may have strong roots. Each twig or bud added to it bears the same kind of fruit as its own parent. Some apple trees bear four or five varieties of fruit on the same plant, because of the different twigs that have been joined to it. The seedless varieties of oranges and grapefruits are also grown in this way.

IMPROVING OUR FRUITS

SOMETIMES something happens by chance within a seed so that it bears a plant that is in some way different from its parents. It is a new variety of the plant. Such a variety is called a *chance seedling*. The McIntosh apple was a chance seedling that was discovered by a farmer in Ontario, Canada. The

McIntosh apple

navel orange, another chance seedling, was found in Brazil. These seedlings were better in some ways than their parent plants.

People can improve plants, too. Plant breeders select extra-good plants that have certain qualities they like. Then they take care that the pollen of one of these plants gets to the flowers of another. Some of the plants that result may have sweeter, juicier fruit, they may be able to resist insects or diseases better, or they may have some other good quality. Twigs of the successful plants are then grafted onto other trees. In this way, new varieties are grown.

Although many of the fruits we eat today were developed fairly recently, many others date back to very ancient times. They began as wild plants, but men gradually learned to cultivate and improve them.

As trade routes were opened, caravans carried goods between countries far distant from each other. Fruit seeds and plants were among their precious cargoes. Conquering soldiers also helped the spread of many kinds of fruits. The Greeks under Alexander the Great brought peaches back from Samarkand in southern Russia. Explorers and travelers have played their part, too. Columbus brought the seeds of the orange to the New World.

Today, because of fast means of transportation and new freezing and canning methods, we can enjoy fruits and fruit juices from many parts of the world. The kinds and varieties of fruits offered in the market are constantly growing. Now many shops sell mangoes, papayas, and sapotes. Some people think of these tropical fruits as luxuries. But oranges were a luxury a little more than sixty years ago. Before long, perhaps, we shall begin our breakfasts or end our dinners with many tropical fruits strange to us now.

THE POME, OR CORE, FRUITS

POME FRUITS belong to the huge plant family named *Rosaceae* (ro-*zay*-see-ee), the Rose family. These fruits have several seeds within a tough, papery chamber we call the core. Apples, pears, and quinces belong to this group. When we eat them, we are actually eating the greatly enlarged flower tubes of the plants.

Baldwin apple

Golden Delicious apple

Apple

The apple is perhaps the king of all fruits. The ancestors of the apple varieties we eat today probably first grew in southeast Asia, around the Caspian and Black seas. From this area they spread across Europe. We know that, during the Stone Age, the ancient lake dwellers ate apples raw. Or they cut, dried, and preserved them for later use. Fossils of apples have been found embedded in mud at the bottom of Swiss lakes and in the burned ruins of the long-ago lake dwellings. These fossils are over five thousand years old.

During the early times when many tasty varieties of apples were being cultivated in central and northern Europe and across parts of Asia, the American continent had only crab apples. These apples were eaten by the Indians, although they are very tart and sour.

Early colonists — English, French, and Dutch — brought apple seeds to North America. Even earlier, the Spaniards brought seeds to Mexico and South America. Within a short time, orchards were thriving in the New World colonies. The Indians planted the fruit, too.

In the 1800's, a missionary named John Chapman roamed from Pennsylvania to Iowa, barefoot and dressed in a grain sack. He took a boatload of apple seeds and seedlings down the Ohio River. Upon landing, he planted apples over hundreds of miles of country, so that the settlers who followed could have orchards. He became known as Johnny Appleseed.

Even today, an old American saying is still repeated: "An apple a day keeps the doctor away." There may be some basis for this belief, as apples are rich in vitamins.

In the spring, an apple tree bursting with pink and white flowers is a lovely sight. Of the more than one thousand apple varieties grown in North America, perhaps twenty-five are outstanding. Among these are the McIntosh, Golden Delicious, Winesap, Baldwin, Gravenstein, Cortland, Northern Spy, Rome Beauty, and Wealthy. Different varieties of apples ripen at different times, from mid-July to late fall. Some varieties can be stored for weeks, even months, while others rot quickly.

Crab apple

We usually picture apples as red, but many varieties are green, and others are yellow or russet. Some have spots, stripes, or blushes of color. Some have thick, waxy skins, while others have skins that are thin and smooth. The inside flesh may range from snowy white, as in the McIntosh, to yellow, as in the Golden Delicious. Some apples are juicy; others are not. Each variety has its own particular "apple" taste, not quite like any other.

Although apple trees may live for a century, most growers replace old trees every forty or fifty years. Usually this is done by selecting a variety and grafting it onto crab apple stock. The United States today produces over 110,000,000 bushels of apples a year. Washington, New York, Michigan, Virginia, and California are the leading states in apple growing.

Pear

The early Swiss lake dwellers, who built their huts on pilings driven into the swampy ground, ate not only apples, but pears. Charred fossil pears have been found on the bottoms of the lakes. When the primitive wooden huts burned, the fruits evidently fell into the water.

The walls of early Egyptian tombs show pictures of pears, and the ancient Greeks even had a pear festival. By A.D. 100, Roman farmers were growing forty-one varieties of pear, according to Pliny, the famous Roman naturalist and writer.

In 1629, pear seeds appeared on a list of items to be sent from England to the Pilgrims in Plymouth. In 1647, a pear tree was planted in New Amsterdam by Dutch colonists. Fifty-eight years later, French settlers were planting pear trees along the banks of the Detroit River.

While European pears were good to eat, their oriental cousin, the sand pear, was not. It was cultivated in China and Japan for its beautiful blossoms. No one ate sand pears because they were gritty and dry.

In 1850, this plant came to America by way of Europe. Years later, Peter Kieffer, a gardener near Philadelphia, noticed that one of his sand pear seedlings had leaves that were different than usual. This seedling had come from a sand pear flower pollinated by Bartlett pear trees growing in an orchard nearby. Kieffer transplanted the tree and cared for it until it bore fruit in 1873. Kieffer pears are still widely grown, but Seckel pears, which also first came from Philadelphia, are much better. They are small, but are famous for their juicy sweetness.

Seckel pear

Bartlett pear

Other well-known pear varieties are the Bartlett and the Bosc, Comice, and Anjou. These last three are "winter pears." They ripen late in the season and keep well in the winter. Pears may be yellow, like a ripened Bartlett, or green, or russet, like a Bosc, or russety red, like a Seckel. Unlike apple trees, pear trees will not withstand very cold winters. The mild-weather states of Oregon, California, and Washington produce the best varieties and the greatest quantities of pears.

Quince

Although some varieties of quince are apple- or orange-shaped, most are pear-shaped. They are about the size of a baseball, and are yellow and slightly hairy. Quince trees grow to be no more than about 20 feet tall, and most of them are smaller.

Quinces were first cultivated in central and eastern Asia, more than two thousand years ago. From there, plants were brought to Europe. The ancient Greeks and Romans liked quinces, and the fruit is often mentioned in their writings. The American colonists ordered quince seeds from England in 1629, along with apple and pear seeds. But quinces are not very popular today because they are hard and sour. They cannot be eaten raw, as an apple or pear

Quince

can, but must be cooked. The fruit makes a delicious jelly, and is also used to flavor other cooked dishes.

The important quince-growing states are California, Ohio, Pennsylvania, and New York.

THE DRUPE, OR STONE, FRUITS

DRUPES are fleshy fruits that have a single seed enclosed in a hard, thick stone. They are often called stone fruits. Like the pome, or core, fruits, they belong to the huge Rose family.

Peach

It is thought that peaches were first cultivated in China over four thousand years ago. Five centuries before Christ, Confucius, the great Chinese thinker, discovered a poem that mentioned them, and wrote it down. That poem dated back to 1800 B.C.

There are many ancient myths about peaches. One tells the story of the Royal Lady of the West, whose garden contained a peach tree that bore fruit once every three thousand years. Anyone who could pick this fruit would live forever.

Chinese merchants were responsible for bringing peaches westward to Persia. Gradually the trees spread to Italy, France, and Spain. The Spanish conquerors brought seeds to Mexico and Central America in the 1500's. By the time the colonists of Jamestown arrived in the New World, peaches had been scattered far and wide by the Indians, and the settlers thought that the peach was a native American fruit tree.

Peach trees have quite short lives — from ten to fifteen years. They are related to the almond, and their lovely pink blossoms appear earlier in the spring than those of most other fruit trees, before the leaves of the tree come out.

Elberta peach

Nectarine

Some peaches are clingstone varieties — the flesh of the fruit clings to the stone. Others are freestones — the flesh comes away from the stone easily. Freestone peaches are the best for eating in the hand, while clingstones are used by commercial canners.

There are hundreds of peach varieties. Among the most popular are the Belle, Elberta, Greensboro, Golden Jubilee, and Honey. A great deal of work is going on among peach growers, to develop even better varieties of the fruit.

Peach trees cannot endure bitterly cold winters, so they must be raised in areas where the climate is not too harsh. The most important peach-growing states are California, Georgia, and Michigan. North Carolina and South Carolina, Colorado, and Utah also have large peach crops.

Nectarines are fuzzless peaches. Their leaves and flowers look like those of a peach, but their fruit is a little smaller and often tastes slightly bitter. Nectarines have been found growing on the same tree as peaches.

Plum

There are several different groups of plums. Among them are the Damson, the European, the American, and the Japanese plums.

Damson plums date back to the Stone Age. Pits of these plums have been found on the sites of prehistoric dwellings. Damsons get their name from the Syrian city of Damascus, where they were grown in abundance for many years. They are dark purple in color, and are generally small and round — about an inch in diameter. Though somewhat sour, they make excellent jam or plum butter.

European plums made their way to America with the Spanish settlers, who planted them around their missions in the Southwest. There are many varieties of European plums. They may be green in color, or yellow or red or purple. Probably the best known is the green-to-yellow Reine Claude (renn clode), which was named after a queen of France. Later, Sir William Gage, an English botanist, introduced this plum into his country, and it was named

13

Damson plum

Native American plum

"greengage" for him. Purple-black Italian prune plums and some other European varieties with firm, meaty flesh are often grown in the United States to be marketed as prunes. After harvesting, they are dried in the sun or in dehydrators and are then given a glossy coating in a steam, fruit-juice, or glycerine bath. In the process they become prunes.

Native American plums did a great deal to liven up the rather dreary diets of the American Indians and the first white settlers. American plums were not good dessert food because they were small and tart, but the colonists cooked them as preserves.

The Indians introduced the colonists to the orange-yellow Canadian plum and to the small purple beach plum. Beach plums still grow wild along the coasts of southern Maine, and abundantly on the beaches of Cape Cod, and southward to Virginia.

Japanese plums originated in China sometime over two thousand years ago. In 1870 a California fruitgrower imported some trees from Japan. Since then, plant breeders have experimented with pollen from the Japanese plum flowers. They have developed many new varieties in combination with some of the native American plums. Now there are over three hundred different kinds of plums.

California, Washington, Oregon, and Idaho all grow large crops of the fruit.

Apricot

The native home of the apricot is probably central or western China. Chinese writings over two thousand years old contain a character which is believed to mean "apricot." Chinese legends tell that Lao-Tse, a great Chinese thinker who lived in the sixth century B.C., was born under an apricot tree and could speak as soon as he was born. Lao-Tse, in ancient Chinese, means "apricot."

The Greeks claimed that Alexander the Great sent the apricot back to his country from Armenia. Hence its botanical name, *Prunus armeniaca* (ar-

15

Apricot

mee-nee-*ay*-ka). From Greece the trees spread through the temperate parts of Europe. The Spaniards brought apricots to the New World, and according to Captain John Smith, the English were growing them in Virginia in 1629.

Apricots look like small orange-yellow peaches. Most Americans know them best when they have been dried or canned or made into fruit juice. Apricots are dried by halving them, removing the pit, and exposing them to the fumes of burning sulphur for two to six hours. Then they are placed in trays in the sun for many days.

Most of the North American crop is raised in California, although apricots are also grown in Washington and Utah.

Cherry

There are over five hundred varieties of cultivated cherries. They can be divided into two main groups: sweet cherries, which are good for eating raw, and sour cherries, which are used in canning and cooking. Another group, the

16

duke cherries, falls halfway between the two, and may have developed from pollination between sweet and sour varieties. Cherries range in color from very dark red, or black, to bright red, to yellow.

The fruit is native to both the Old and New worlds. Old World cherries first grew in Asia Minor. From there, birds carried the seeds into Europe. We know that Stone Age people ate cherries, for the pits have been found in their refuse piles.

About 300 B.C., the Greek writer Theophrastus, one of the earliest botanists, described the tree and fruit of the sour cherry. Later, Pliny the Elder, a Roman author of the first century, wrote about ten different varieties of the fruit growing in Italy, and noted that cherries had been taken to Britain. Columbus, and the Spanish colonists who came later, brought the fruit to Florida and the West Indies, where it did not survive, because cherries like a cool climate. But the English colonists, only nine years after they settled in Massachusetts, had good luck in growing the sweet Red Kentish cherry.

Cherries moved westward with the settlers. In 1847, Henderson Luelling took an assortment of seven hundred fruit plants to Oregon in seven ox-drawn wagons. One of the covered wagons carried small cherry trees. It is said that this pioneer fruitgrower started the great sweet cherry industry on the Pacific Coast.

Montmorency cherry

Bing cherry

Sour cherries can endure colder winters and more rain than sweet cherries can. They thrive in the northern half of the United States, as far west as the Great Lakes region. Sweet cherries need a fairly even and mild climate. The Great Lakes and Pacific Coast regions are good for this crop.

BUSH FRUITS AND STRAWBERRIES

BECAUSE OF THEIR names, we think of some of the fruits in this chapter as berries. Strawberries, raspberries, and blackberries are not really berries, but aggregate fruits, as was explained earlier in this book.

Raspberry and Blackberry

Some very prickly bushes or shrubs are called *brambles*. Raspberries, blackberries, and their relatives grow on such bushes and because of this are often called *bramble fruits*. These members of the Rose family have spiny stalks with soft, pithy centers.

Blackberries differ from raspberries in that their thorny stems are much more dangerous to the berry picker. And when a blackberry is ripe, both the fruit and the softened receptacle, or core, that it clings to are eaten.

On the other hand, the raspberry's receptacle remains hard even when the fruit is ripe. When the fruit is picked, the berry slips off, leaving the hard core behind on the bush.

18

Blackberries and raspberries are natives of Asia, Europe, and North America. They can be grown from the Equator to the Arctic Ocean. Pliny, the ancient Roman naturalist, wrote that the Greeks called raspberries *Idae* because they grew on Mount Ida, in Crete. So, when the famous botanist Linnaeus worked out a system for giving plants Latin names, he called the European raspberry *Rubus idaeus* — "the red berry of Mount Ida."

Raspberries grew wild until the 1600's, when they first came under cultivation. The colonists who brought European varieties to America found both red and black raspberries already growing abundantly in the forest clearings.

Some blackberries grow on tall, thorny stalks. Others are trailing types, often called dewberries. When the slender canes of trailing blackberries touch the soil, they root at the tips and form new plants.

Three trailing blackberries are now grown widely: the youngberry, the boysenberry — a chance seedling found in California — and the loganberry.

Eskimos and Indians of northern Canada eat cloudberries, a kind of trailing raspberry. It is an unusually hardy plant that will produce fruit even as far north as the Arctic Circle. Because of their amber or golden color when ripe, cloudberries are often called yellowberries by the people of northern Quebec and the Hudson Bay area.

Red raspberry

Blackberry

Strawberry

Strawberry

Raspberries and blackberries grow on bushes, but not the strawberry. It is the fruit of a low-growing herb. Strawberry plants produce many runners. When they touch the soil, these runners root at the tips. In this way new plants are formed. The berry that we eat is really an enlarged, fleshy part of the flower stalk, the receptacle. The tiny brown seeds are embedded in its surface.

Strawberries have grown wild over much of Europe since very early times, but they were not cultivated until the fifteenth century. In America the early colonists discovered an abundance of wild strawberries. A Maryland settler wrote, "Wee cannot sett downe a foote but tred on strawberries." Although the American berries tasted better than the European ones, they were still small and quite dry.

In 1712 a Frenchman, Captain Frezier, arrived in France with four or five strawberry plants, all that had survived a six-month sea voyage. These plants, from Chile, produced luscious big strawberries. Later, both French and English gardeners grew the Chilean plants beside those from eastern North America. The fruits that came from an exchange of pollen between the two kinds of flowers produced fine crops of large, juicy berries.

Today, strawberries are grown in every state of the United States. Many of the berries are the much improved descendants of the earlier Chilean and North American plants. The leading strawberry-growing states are Florida, Louisiana, Tennessee, Missouri, Kentucky, Arkansas, Illinois, Oregon, Michigan, Washington, California, and North Carolina.

Currant and Gooseberry

Currants and gooseberries are true berries. They belong to the Saxifrage family. These two fruits are native to the colder parts of North America and Europe, but are not nearly as popular in the United States as they are in northern Europe, especially in England. Because they are sour, they are used mostly for pies, jams and preserves, and sometimes for puddings.

Gooseberry

Currant

Some varieties of gooseberry and currant bushes harbor a fungus, the white pine blister rust. In order to live, this fungus must spend one-half its life on currant or gooseberry bushes and the other half on white pine trees. Because white pines are killed by the rust, many states forbid the cultivation of currants and gooseberries. In this way the rust is destroyed.

Although wild currants date back to prehistoric times, they were not cultivated in Europe until the Middle Ages. Because they were better than the native American berries, European currants were brought to Plymouth Colony in America in 1629.

When William Clark and Meriwether Lewis explored the West in the years from 1804 to 1806 they found that the Indians ate the black currants that grew wild along the Missouri and Columbia rivers. The explorers brought these so-called buffalo currants back east, to be raised in gardens.

Currant fruits may be red, yellow, or greenish-white in color, depending on the variety.

Unlike the smooth-stemmed currant bushes, gooseberry shoots and canes bristle with mean thorns. The history of both fruits is quite similar, however. By the time Columbus discovered America, both berries were garden grown in the Netherlands, Germany, and England. Both were brought to America by the Pilgrims. But the imported gooseberries were easily attacked by a mildew disease. Only the native gooseberry plants did not have this trouble. Finally a plant breeder crossed wild American plants with European stock and produced a new variety of gooseberry that resisted the disease.

Gooseberries are about the size of marbles. They may be red, white, or green-white when ripe. Their color depends on the variety of the plant.

HEATH FRUITS

THE HEATH FAMILY and its relatives include many woody plants such as heather, mountain laurel, rhododendron, and azalea, in addition to blueberry, huckleberry, and cranberry. Members of this huge family grow on heaths — somewhat open, swampy places — shady woodlands, or rock-strewn slopes.

Blueberry

Blueberries, like many of their heath relatives, grow in an acid soil. This type of soil is made of rotting vegetation and is often found deep in the woods. When farmers cut down and burn off their woodland acres, the blueberry is one of the first plants to spring up thereafter.

Blueberries are natives of the northern part of the globe, and even grow in Alaska. In the eastern part of the United States, wild blueberries can be divided into two groups: highbush and lowbush. Highbush blueberries grow to heights of from six to ten feet. Lowbush blueberries may grow as high as two feet.

In 1909, the botanist Dr. Frederick V. Coville and his associates in New Jersey began offering cash awards for highbush blueberry plants bearing particularly large fruit. From these some eighteen new varieties were developed, some of which are now cultivated. Their fruit is often more than double the size of the original wild berries.

In Maine, wild lowbush blueberries growing thickly on the heaths, or "barrens," have been partially cultivated and are harvested as an important crop.

Although various kinds of blueberries are found all over Asia, Europe, and North and South America, only Canada and the United States grow them on a large scale. New Jersey, Michigan, North Carolina, and Maine are leaders in production.

Blueberry

Huckleberry

Huckleberries look much like blueberries, and amateurs often confuse the two. It is easy to tell the difference if you look for a bloom — or light, powdery-blue coating on the berry. Blueberries have this. Huckleberries often do not; they are usually shiny and dark blue. Huckleberries have ten somewhat bony seeds, while blueberries have many tiny seeds.

While blueberries are true berries, huckleberries are berry-like drupes. They are not grown as a crop, for their fruit is not nearly as good as that of the blueberry.

Cranberry

I-bimi, meaning "bitter berries," was an Indian name for cranberries. Until the Indians showed the colonists how to cook them, the Pilgrims at Plymouth had little use for these bright red berries growing on short woody vines. One Indian recipe called for pounded, dried meat mixed with *i-bimi*; this produced a food called pemmican. Although some people claim that a cranberry sauce was eaten at the first Thanksgiving dinner in October, 1621, no one really knows.

The American cranberry is native from Nova Scotia to North Carolina and westward to Wisconsin. Cape Cod, in Massachusetts, is a great cranberry-raising center. Until 1816, the berries were not cultivated, but were picked wild. Then Henry Hall transplanted wild vines to a bog on his land in Dennis, on Cape Cod. Sixteen years later he was producing about seventy bushels of cranberries on each acre of land. Today, because of careful selection, an acre of land can produce three hundred bushels of fruit.

Cranberries grow best in a low bog that can be flooded to protect the vines from winter frosts and to control insect pests at other times during the growing season.

Cranberry

To grow cranberries, all vegetation in the bog must first be burned off, or destroyed by flooding the land for two years. Then a dam with floodgates is built, and the vine cuttings are planted in a shallow layer of sand. Two or three years go by before a bog produces berries in any quantity.

Cranberries are usually harvested with large rake-toothed scoops, which, when pulled through the vines, remove the berries. One early method of sorting or grading berries was to roll them down a series of ten to thirty steps. Good berries bounded to the bottom, while the soft, inferior ones stayed on the steps. Today, picking machines are used in some bogs, and nearly all grading is done by machinery.

Cranberry growing is centered in Massachusetts, Wisconsin, New Jersey, Washington, and Oregon. Most of the cranberry harvest is sold canned, as sauce or juice.

THE MULBERRY FAMILY

THE PLANTS in the mulberry family are woody and have a milky juice. Many are tropical. In other ways, the members of this family do not seem much alike. One member is a tree that produces rubber; another gives us figs; a third bears breadfruit; a fourth produces mulberries. Still other family relatives are trees of ornamental value only.

26

Mulberry

The fruits of the mulberry tree are not true berries, but are multiple fruits. That is, each fruit is formed by the ripened ovaries of several flowers, grown together into one mass. Mulberry trees may grow to a height of 60 feet and are sometimes found near old farms. Because the fruit is too fragile to keep or ship, it is seldom sold in the markets. The berries drop to the ground when ripe, and are eaten mostly by animals and birds.

In the eastern section of the United States there are three kinds of mulberry: red, white, and black. The red, or American, mulberry, is a native, and grows from New England to Texas.

White mulberries are natives of Asia. Their fruit is edible, but extremely sweet. The mulberry leaves are most important, though, because they are the food of silkworms. White mulberry cuttings were taken to Italy in 1434. The Italians soon discovered that their silkworms preferred these leaves to those of the black mulberry, which had been growing in Italy since about A.D. 500.

In 1623, the American colonists in Virginia imported mulberries and silkworm eggs from Europe in an attempt to develop a silkmaking industry in America. The plants thrived and spread throughout the South, but the silkworms died.

In tropical areas of the South Pacific, the people produce tapa cloth from the soaked and pounded bark of the paper mulberry. The Japanese turn the bark into large sheets of paper. These are attached to sliding window and door frames, or to screens that are used as room dividers.

Mulberry

Fig

The story of fig trees goes back almost to the beginning of history. The Bible states that figs grew in the Garden of Eden, and that fig leaves were the first clothing of Adam and Eve. The ancient Egyptians cultivated figs, and the fruit became popular on the island of Crete some thirty-five hundred years ago. Figs were grown also by the ancient Greeks and Romans. The Spanish missionaries brought fig trees to North America about four hundred and fifty years ago.

The fruit of the fig tree is made of a fleshy receptacle — the fattened-out end of a flower stalk. Inside this hollow receptacle are scores of tiny flowers, which bloom in complete darkness. At one end of the receptacle is a very small opening through which a tiny pollen-laden wasp can enter. The wasp pollinates the female fig flowers, which then develop seeds.

Only one kind of wasp can pollinate the flowers of some kinds of figs. This small wasp lays its eggs in the flowers of a wild fig variety, the caprifig. When the wasps are hatched and grown, they leave the wild fig flowers and often fly to the cultivated fig trees. In so doing, they carry the wild fig pollen with them.

Caprifig trees are useless except that they house the wasps and provide an abundance of pollen. Owners of fig orchards often place in their trees small baskets of the caprifig flowers containing the fig wasps.

In the late 1800's, Smyrna fig plants were taken to California. Although the trees grew well, their fruit was small, and dropped to the ground unripened. Finally it was discovered that the Smyrna fig would not develop unless it was pollinated by the caprifig wasp. When both wild trees and wasps were imported and became plentiful, the Smyrna fig trees produced large, luscious fruit.

Smyrna, Kassaba, and Mission figs are good eating when dried. Kadota figs are usually canned, while Turkey figs are mostly eaten fresh. Fresh ripe figs may be green in color, or they may vary from yellow to brown, or purple to black.

28

Fig

Because of their climate, California and Texas are the leading fig-producing states, although some varieties of fig may grow as far north as Michigan or New Jersey.

Breadfruit

Breadfruit

The breadfruit is probably a native of Malaya, but long ago it was carried from one island to another by the seafaring Polynesians, and is now spread widely through the South Pacific isles.

Breadfruit trees often grow to a height of fifty feet. Their handsome, leathery leaves, curious flowers, and huge, rough fruits are a familiar sight on many tropical islands. Ripened breadfruits are yellow and are often as big as melons.

This useful fruit has played a strange part in history. In 1788 the King of England became interested in transplanting breadfruit trees from the Pacific to the West Indies. He sent Captain William Bligh in the ship *Bounty* to Tahiti, to pick up some breadfruit seedlings. With the seedlings on board, the *Bounty* sailed for Jamaica in April, 1789. But Bligh was a tyrant, and soon his crew mutinied. The captain and eighteen other men were put to sea in an open boat, while the mutineers settled on Pitcairn Island. To this day we know of this dramatic incident as "the mutiny on the *Bounty*." Later, Captain Bligh did carry breadfruit plants to the West Indies, but they have never been as important there as in their native Pacific.

30

Primarily breadfruit is eaten as a vegetable. Dried breadfruit pulp may be ground into flour and baked as bread. Some breadfruit varieties are baked or roasted, and taste much like potatoes would if they were cooked with large amounts of sugar and milk. Breadfruit bark, like that of the mulberry, may be pounded and made into cloth.

THE GRAPE FAMILY

THERE ARE over five hundred kinds of plants in the Grape family. Many of these are vines, trees, and shrubs of the tropics, but some of them are woody vines that grow in the temperate zone. These vines climb by means of tiny curling stems called tendrils. The tendrils reach out and wrap themselves around wires, posts, tree branches, and whatever else they may touch, holding the vine in place as it climbs. Two relatives of the grape are the Virginia creeper and the Boston ivy. These plants are cultivated for their lovely foliage.

Grape

The Norsemen who came to America about five hundred years before Columbus found so many wild grapevines that they called the country Vinland. The early settlers of Virginia saw great vines climbing on trees everywhere. They were probably the vines of the fox grape. From this plant many fine American grapes, including the Concord and Niagara, were later developed. As wild American grapes were not as good in some ways as the European kinds, the colonists imported Old World vines. But these were plagued by diseases and pests which did not attack the native American grapes found growing along the Atlantic Coast.

Although Old World grapes failed to grow in the eastern colonies, they thrived around the missions established by the Spaniards in the late 1500's in what is now New Mexico. In 1769, Spanish missions in California began planting the Old World grapes. Now California has become the greatest

Concord grape

White Seedless grape

grape-producing area in the Americas. Today that state grows about three million tons of grapes a year. But this is only about 10 per cent of the world's grape supply. Grape growing is the largest fruit industry in the world.

About one hundred years ago, an insect called the root louse was accidentally taken to Europe. This native of the eastern part of the United States nearly destroyed the European vineyards. Fortunately, scientists discovered that it did not attack the Old World vines if they were grafted onto the roots of American grapes. Today many vineyards throughout the world are partly or wholly made up of vines grown on roots of American stock.

When they are dried, certain varieties of grapes become raisins. Muscat, Sultana, and the pale-green Thompson Seedless grapes make some of the finest raisins. Table grapes include Thompson Seedless, Tokay, Malaga, Muscat, Emperor, and Ribier. In the Northeast, and other cool sections of the United States, the popular varieties are Concord, Catawba, Delaware, and Fredonia. Wine making in the United States is centered in California and New York. Several of the grape varieties mentioned above are grown for wines, and there are other wine grapes. A number of the American varieties make very fine grape juice, jams, and jellies, too.

THE CITRUS FRUITS

CITRUS FRUITS need subtropical or tropical climates. The word "citrus" is the ancient Latin name for the citron tree, the oldest citrus fruit tree known to Europeans. Citron peel is preserved to be used in making plum puddings and fruitcakes.

Citrus fruits grow on evergreen shrubs and trees which have dark-green, glossy leaves and very fragrant flowers, mostly white. The nectar from these blossoms produces a fine honey. The fruits are really large berries that have a heavy peel, or rind, beneath which is a juicy flesh. This flesh is divided into many sections by thin, tough membranes. Each section contains one or more seeds, except in the seedless varieties. The rind is oily and bitter-tasting.

33

Orange

Oranges are native to South China and Indochina, where they have grown for more than four thousand years. During ancient times they spread to India, and then, about eleven hundred years ago, to Persia. Not until the fifteenth century were sweet oranges mentioned in European writings. On his second voyage across the Atlantic, Columbus brought orange seeds and those of other citrus fruits from the Canary Islands to Hispaniola, in the Caribbean Sea.

The Spanish conquerors of the Aztecs cultivated orange trees around their new estates near present-day Mexico City, and when the Spaniards settled in Florida they planted orange trees. In 1764, one grove of wild oranges was found to be forty miles long. When Florida became a state in 1845, orange growing became a business. Today Florida is one of the leading orange-growing regions of the world.

In 1769, sweet oranges were planted at the San Diego mission in California. From there they spread to other missions, and now California is another important orange-growing region.

There are three kinds of oranges, each with many varieties. The sweet orange has round to oval fruit with a peel that clings to the pulp. The smaller mandarin orange or the tangerine has skin that separates easily from the pulp.

Navel orange

The sour or bitter orange cannot be eaten out of hand, but is used for marmalade, and for orangeade drinks.

Oranges are a wonderful source of vitamin C, and so are valuable in a person's diet. Besides the fresh fruit, great amounts of orange juice are sold, both canned and frozen.

Oranges are grown in all tropical and subtropical countries, but principally in the United States, Spain, Brazil, Japan, Italy, Argentina, Mexico, Egypt, Republic of South Africa, Paraguay, Algeria, and Palestine. Plant scientists have been able to develop several new types of oranges. Crossing sweet oranges and tangerines produced tangors. Tangelos are a cross between grapefruit and sweet oranges.

The navel orange came from a chance seedling found in Brazil. Two young trees of this variety were sent to California in 1873. Navel oranges have since become California's principal winter orange crop.

Grapefruit

The ancestor of the grapefruit is the pomelo. This large, coarse, thick-skinned fruit is thought to be a native of the Malay Archipelago and nearby islands. During the late 1600's, Captain Shaddock, commander of an East Indian trading ship, brought some pomelo seeds to the island of Barbados, near South America. The seeds grew, and the fruit became known as the shaddock.

A book called *The Natural History of Barbados,* published in 1750, listed the shaddock under the name "forbidden fruit." The name "grapefruit" originated in Jamaica, an island in the West Indies. Scientists believe that at some point the shaddock produced a chance seedling or that it was crossed with a sweet orange. In any case, the grapefruit of today is far better for eating than its original ancestor was. It is smaller and thinner-skinned and juicier. It received its name because the fruit grows in large grapelike clusters on the tree.

In the early 1800's a Spanish nobleman planted grapefruit trees on his

Grapefruit

estate in Florida, but it was not until around 1880 that the fruit was raised commercially. About ten years later, a tree with nearly seedless fruit was discovered near Lakeland, Florida. This tree was the beginning of the popular Marsh variety we buy in the market today. Still later, a pink-fleshed, nearly seedless variety was discovered. Scientists have improved these and other varieties in many ways. Today a single tree, for example, can produce 1,500 pounds of fruit a year.

Florida, Texas, Arizona, and California now grow about two million tons of grapefruit annually.

Lemon and Lime

The lemon and the lime are very close relatives, with histories that are much alike. Both originated in the warm regions of Burma and India. Both produce sweet varieties of fruit that are prized by oriental peoples, but remain unpopular with Americans and Europeans. American markets sell only sour lemons and sour limes. Both lemons and limes are yellow when ripe, but limes are commonly sold while still green. Both fruits are used in making cool drinks and for flavoring foods.

Lemons have been known in the Mediterranean region since the days of the ancient Greeks and Romans. The Arabs grew lemons and limes in Persia and Palestine long before the Crusades, and Arabs brought the fruits into Spain in the twelfth century.

Columbus, on his second voyage to the New World, brought the seeds of the lemon and lime to Hispaniola. During the early years of the sixteenth century the Spanish conquerors of Mexico and Central America set out the trees on their estates. In 1565, Spanish settlers planted lemons and limes at St. Augustine, Florida. Unfortunately, because these fruits are easily damaged by frost and extreme heat, they have not grown well in Florida. Lemons are now grown in southern California. Argentina, Chile, Spain, Greece, Sicily, and Turkey also produce large lemon crops.

Because limes can withstand heat and humidity better than lemons, they are now widely cultivated in the West Indies and in the lowlands of Mexico. Egypt is the world's leading producer of both sweet and sour limes.

Back in sailing ship days, British sailors were required to drink a daily dose of lime juice. This prevented the dreaded disease, scurvy, which was caused by the lack of fresh fruit and vegetables on long voyages. Now we realize that the vitamin C in lime juice was the important thing in preventing the disease. Even today, Englishmen are sometimes jokingly referred to as limeys, because of that old British sailing ship tradition.

Lemon   Tahiti lime

THE GOURD FAMILY

MELONS are members of the Gourd family. Besides watermelons and musk-melons, this large family includes pumpkins, squashes, gourds, and cucumbers. All these plants are vines that creep along the ground and have large, rather fuzzy leaves.

Watermelon

The fruit of the watermelon is berry-like. It has a hard rind, which remains green even when the fruit is ripe. The pulp of the ripe fruit is pink to red, very watery, and has many seeds.

Watermelons are natives of Africa, where they were first cultivated by ancient tribes. Much later, they were grown in Egypt. And later still, the seeds were carried to the Near East and across Asia to China. The New World colonists had brought seeds with them and were trying to grow watermelons in Massachusetts in 1629. Apparently the Indians obtained seeds, for French explorers found that some of the tribes of the Mississippi Valley were raising watermelons. Many seeds were also no doubt brought directly from Africa on the slave ships that soon made regular voyages to the New World.

Watermelon

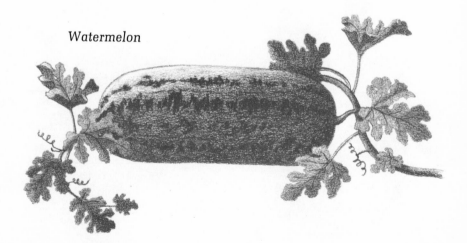

Muskmelon

Honeydew melon

Persian melon

Casaba melon

All of the watermelon is good to eat. The rinds make excellent pickles and preserves, and the seeds are often cooked and eaten in Mexico and Europe. One variety, the citron melon, is grown only for pickling and preserving, and is added to many jams and jellies.

Watermelons prefer a warm climate, and grow better in the southern part of the United States than in the north. Georgia, Florida, California, South Carolina, and Texas are the leading watermelon-producing states.

Muskmelon

This fruit probably originated in Persia, but today muskmelons are grown in warm and temperate climates everywhere. There are three principal kinds: nutmeg, or netted, melons; cantaloupes; and winter melons, such as the honeydews, Persians, and casabas.

Nutmeg melons have netted, ribbed skins and orange flesh. The melons we find in the markets and mistakenly call cantaloupes are really nutmeg melons. True cantaloupes, commonly grown in Europe, have a hard rind and are warty and scaly.

Muskmelons were probably known to the ancient Egyptians; melons seem to be pictured in their wall paintings. The Roman naturalist, Pliny, described them in his book, *Natural History*. Columbus brought muskmelon seeds to the Caribbean islands in 1494. Later travelers brought seeds to Mexico and to the early North American colonies.

Casaba, Persian, and Crenshaw melons — the winter melons — generally have green or white flesh, although there are some that have orange flesh. Their rinds do not have ribbed sections. In fact, the honeydew's pale green to cream-colored rind is very smooth. These melons ripen late in the season and can be shipped and stored for longer periods of time than nutmeg melons can.

Today, California, Arizona, Texas, South Carolina, North Carolina, Arkansas, Colorado, Indiana, Michigan, Missouri, Georgia, Maryland, and New Jersey are important muskmelon-growing states.

40

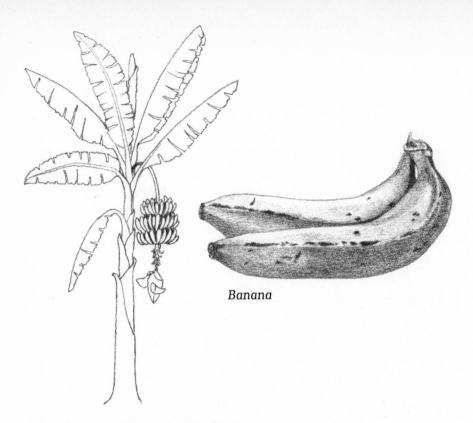

Banana

THE BANANA FAMILY

THE MEMBERS OF the Banana family are the largest herbs in the world. Although they look like trees, they are not. Their trunks are really leafstalks rolled tightly together. Among the members of this family are the bird-of-paradise flower, cultivated for its strikingly beautiful blossoms, and the Manila hemp, whose fiber is used for making rope. Probably the best-known member of the family is the banana itself.

Banana

Bananas have been known since very early times. They are natives of southeast Asia, and thrive in hot, rainy climates. The banana fruits are really

41

long berries, which contain little black specks that are undeveloped seeds.

Banana plants spring up very rapidly. As soon as a plant has borne fruit, it dies down or is cut down, and a new tightly coiled leafstalk springs up from its base. It becomes several feet tall and has three or four leaves in only a few days. Banana leaves are from five to ten feet long and are often used for thatching huts. They fray easily in the tropical winds and always have a tattered appearance. A banana leaf makes an excellent umbrella during a sudden tropical downpour.

Each banana plant has a single spike of blossoms. The flower stalk develops from the root, and pushes its way up the hollow stem, coming out at the crown of the tree. From the blossoms of this spike a bunch of bananas develops. This bunch may weigh anywhere from 80 to 140 pounds. It is made up of many clusters, known as hands. Each hand has from ten to twenty individual bananas, known as fingers.

When bananas are thoroughly ripe, they are very nourishing. Many peoples in tropical countries depend on them as a valuable food. The fruits we buy are picked and shipped while they are still green. When a complete stalk is hung to ripen in the market, it is really upside down.

Although northern markets sell mostly the yellow varieties, there are red, pink, purple, green, and tan bananas. In addition, there is a cooking banana called a plantain. It is green-skinned when ripe. Plantains are baked, fried, or boiled, and are a staple food for poor people living in the tropics.

Bananas are one of the principal products of the Central American countries and are widely grown in the West Indies, Mexico, and Colombia.

THE PINEAPPLE FAMILY

IN PARTS OF the southern United States, long, gray, fluffy moss often hangs draped from live oaks, cypress trees, and even telephone wires. This plant, Spanish moss, is a curious cousin of the pineapple. Of the many groups of plants in the Pineapple family, a number are air plants — that is, they grow on other plants or objects and get their moisture and nutrients from the rain and air. Many of them are raised as houseplants for their brilliantly colored flowers or handsome leaves.

Pineapple

The pineapple is a native of South America. From there it spread to the West Indies, where the European explorers found the Indians growing it. In Brazil and Paraguay the Guaraní Indians' name for it was "anana," which means "excellent fruit." But, because of its appearance, the early Spanish explorers called it *piña de los Indies*, or "pine cone of the Indies." The Spanish and Portuguese carried the plant to Europe and soon it spread to Asia, the East Indies, and Africa. The English named the plant "pineapple."

The fruit is a multiple one, formed from the heavy heads of tiny, purplish flowers springing from the flower stalk and crowned by a tuft of leaves. Each flower becomes a small juicy berry, and all of them are packed solidly together around a large core, or cone. Pineapples take two years to produce their

Pineapple

fruit, which must ripen on the plant. New pineapples are grown either from shoots taken from the mother plant, or from the spiky crown of leaves that is attached to the top of the fruit itself.

In the early 1700's a wealthy merchant in the Netherlands grew pineapples in his greenhouse. His hobby soon spread throughout Europe. Today, fast ships and planes speed the fruit from the tropics and it is no longer necessary to grow pineapples under glass. About four-fifths of the pineapples raised for market come from Hawaii. The fruit is shipped fresh, canned, or as juice. Cuba, Puerto Rico, and the Central American countries also grow large crops of pineapples.

The swordlike leaves of the pineapple contain a coarse fiber that can be made into rope. Finer fibers are made into a cloth called piña, a popular fabric in the Philippine Islands.

THE PALM FAMILY

MANY OF the noblest plants in the tropical world belong to the Palm family. We call them palm *trees*, but they do not have tough, woody trunks like northern trees do. Instead, their trunks are soft, rather like enormous cornstalks, and are topped by a cluster of large leaves. On some kinds of palms the leaves may be 50 feet long. They may be divided into smaller parts, so that they have a feathery look or, on other kinds of palms, the leaves may be fan-shaped. Of the over four thousand kinds of palms, many are used for fiber, lumber, drugs, food, and as ornaments. The three most important palms are the date, coconut, and African oil palm.

Date

The date palm is one of the oldest known food-producing plants. No one is sure of its origin, but the people of ancient Egypt, Babylonia, and Arabia cultivated the plant — it has been cultivated in the Near East for thousands of years. Wild date trees no longer exist.

44

Date

Date palms grow only in hot, dry climates, but their roots must have plenty of water. They are commonly raised around oases in the deserts of Africa and Southwest Asia. There they can "keep their feet wet," while the hot sun ripens their fruit. They do not thrive where there is even a small amount of rainfall.

The date palm may grow to a height of 100 feet and bear fruit for one hundred years. The tree has a shaggy trunk, often made rough by the woody bases of old leaves which have long since broken off. The leaves are feather-like. The fruit is a one-seed berry. It is borne in bunches on stalks that bend downward. There are ten to twelve bunches on a tree, and each has over one thousand single fruits. A bunch of dates may weigh up to forty pounds.

New plants are grown from suckers that shoot out at the base of the trunk. The Spanish missionaries raised dates around their missions in the American Southwest before 1800, but date-growing on a commercial scale began in America in 1890 when the United States Department of Agriculture imported potted palms from Egypt. Now the desert valleys of California and Arizona produce about 20 million pounds of dates a year. At times, helicopters fly over the palms to fan away moisture so that the fruit will ripen properly.

In the hot desert countries of Africa and Asia the date palm is used for many things besides its fruit. The trunk serves as timber; the leaves are excellent thatch for roofs; the fiber is made into rope; and parts of the tree are put to hundreds of other uses.

Coconut

The coconut is one of the most useful plants known to mankind. Its smooth gray trunk is often 100 feet tall, usually without any branches. The outer part is used for timber. The leaves, from 12 to 18 feet long, grow in an open crown at the top of the tree. They can be braided into fans, hats, and baskets, and can also be used for thatching houses. The juice from the flower

Coconut

spike is sometimes made into an alcoholic drink, or into sugar or vinegar. The fruit, which is not really a nut, but a drupe, is covered with a husk. This husk is made of fibers that do not decay readily in salt water and so are used for making fishing nets, for caulking boats, and also for making doormats, rope, and brushes. Inside the husk is the so-called nut. Its shell is often used as a drinking vessel by the natives of tropical islands.

The nut is really a huge seed that contains a solid white meat and a watery fluid or "milk." The meat is eaten fresh or, more often, dried. Shredded coconut meat is often used in candy, pies, cookies, and cakes. When dried nut meats, called copra, are pressed they yield coconut oil, which is added to shampoos, shaving creams, soaps, cooking fats, and oleomargarine. Once the oil has been pressed out, the nut meats form cakes that are sold as cattle food.

Coconuts grow in the East and West Indies, in tropical America, and on the tropical South Pacific islands, where they are often an important food. In the United States they are found in southern California and Florida.

No one is sure where the coconut plant originated. Some botanists say it first grew in the Malay Peninsula and that as the natives journeyed on seafaring expeditions they carried the nuts to other places. Others think that the plant is a native of South America. Because their husks protect the coconuts from salt water, they are hardy travelers. They may drop from a tree into the ocean and float for thousands of miles, to be washed ashore on another tropical beach. There they sprout and grow. After eight to ten years, they begin to bear fruit. Each palm will produce from forty to fifty coconuts a year.

THE EBONY FAMILY

Persimmon

Persimmons are members of the Ebony family. They grow on trees that may be 40 or 50 feet tall, and sometimes even taller. They have thick leaves that are shiny dark green on top, paler underneath. The round fruits are

Persimmon

yellow-orange to red berries with from three to eight flat seeds, and they are about the size of a peach. Two kinds of persimmons are grown in the United States: the common, or American, persimmon, which is found from Connecticut to Iowa and southward; and the Japanese persimmon, which is grown in the warm South and in California. The Japanese persimmon may really be a native of China. It was first brought to the United States sometime after Admiral Perry's visit to Japan in 1853.

After the settling of Jamestown in 1607, Captain John Smith wrote about the American persimmon: "The fruit is . . . green, then yellow and red when it ripens; if it is not ripe it will drive a man's mouth awrie with much torment; but when it is ripe, it is as delicious as an apricock [apricot]."

Persimmons contain an acid, tannin, and unless they are absolutely ripe, the fruit puckers the mouth and makes it feel as if it were trying to turn inside out.

49

THE POMEGRANATE FAMILY

POMEGRANATE TREES have a shrubby appearance, although sometimes they may grow to be 30 feet tall. The fruit is really a berry, about the size and shape of an apple. As a pomegranate ripens, its smooth, leathery skin turns from brownish-yellow to red.

The yellow or reddish pulp is divided into sections which usually contain a mass of small, hard seeds. Some new varieties of the fruit are seedless, however. Pomegranates are eaten raw or as juice.

This is one of the oldest cultivated fruits. It is native to the Middle East. The Egyptians grew it over three thousand years ago, and pomegranate growing spread early to India and China. The ancient Carthaginians grew the fruit, and when the Romans conquered their city in 146 B.C. they brought back to Rome "apples of Carthage," as they called them. The Spaniards carried this fruit to Mexico and California, but it has never become popular in America. In the United States, pomegranates are grown in California, New Mexico, and Arizona. In the South they are often planted for their showy orange-red flowers.

FRUITS POPULAR IN OTHER PARTS OF THE WORLD

Papaya

Although it looks like a tree, the fast-growing papaya is really a giant herb. The plant may grow to a height of 25 feet. At the top of its unbranched main trunk is a crown of leaves. Directly below this hang the fruits, which may weigh up to fifteen pounds each.

The papaya is sometimes called a tree melon because both its appearance and its taste are somewhat like those of a melon. As it ripens, the fruit turns from green to orange-yellow.

The young leaves of the male plant may be cooked and eaten. Sometimes

50

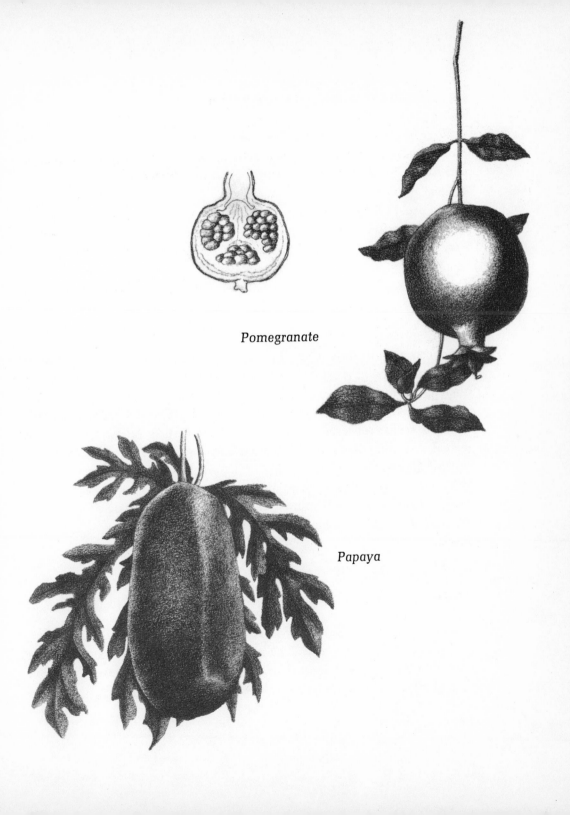

Pomegranate

Papaya

papaya leaves are used as a substitute for soap, as they make a suds when they are rubbed in water.

West Indian cooks wrap papaya leaves around meat to make it tender. The green papaya fruit and the black seeds produce a substance called papain, which aids digestion and is sometimes used in medicine and as a meat tenderizer.

The papaya is a native of tropical America. When the Spanish conquerors invaded America, they found that the Incas of Peru and the Aztecs of Mexico were growing papayas. Later this delicious fruit was carried to other tropical countries.

Loquat

Loquats are members of the Rose family. The loquat fruits are borne on evergreen trees that grow from 20 to 40 feet tall. The trees' thick leaves are often a foot long and are hairy on the undersides. Loquat fruits grow in loose clusters and resemble small yellow plums or pears. They are juicy and have a delicious acid-sweet taste all their own. Their flesh is yellow and contains several dark shiny seeds. In the Mediterranean region of Europe this fruit is called the Japanese medlar.

Loquats are probably native to the mountainous area of southeastern China. They grow best in a warmish climate, and are an important fruit crop in Japan. California has some loquat orchards, and the fruit is also grown in Florida.

Mango

Mangoes are members of the Sumac family, which also includes poison ivy, poison oak, and poison sumac. The "apple of the tropics," the mango, grows on handsome evergreen trees that are sometimes 100 feet tall. They have dark, shiny green leaves.

Loquat

Mango

There are many varieties of mango fruits, which differ greatly in size, color, and shape. Generally they are yellow to red in color, but some kinds are green and others are purple. They hang down from the twigs on long stems.

A mango may be smaller than a peach or it may weigh over three pounds. Some kinds are round, while others are kidney-shaped. Mangoes must be peeled, because the thick skin is quite poisonous and causes swelling and stinging if it touches the mouth. The pulp is sweet and juicy, and has a faint smell like turpentine. In its center is a large, hard pit. Mangoes are eaten raw or are made into jam. Green mangoes are used to make chutney.

The mango tree is a native of southeast Asia and has been grown in India for more than four thousand years. It now is found widely throughout the tropics. In the United States the fruit can be grown successfully only in southern Florida and California.

Guava

The guava is better known as a jelly or preserve fruit than as one to be eaten raw. It is richer in vitamin C than oranges are. This fruit is a true berry that grows on a bushy tree about 20 feet high. From two to four inches long, the fruit is round or pear-shaped, and is yellow when ripe. Beneath its thick skin is a pulp which is whitish-yellow or pinkish, with many seeds. When it is

Guava

Sapodilla

eaten fresh, a guava has a musky flavor, but this taste disappears when the fruit is cooked.

The common guava is a member of the Myrtle family and is a native of tropical America. It has a close relative, the strawberry guava. This fruit is nearly round, purplish-red, and about one inch long. Its pulp is white and tastes a good deal like strawberries. "White" guavas are grown in Florida and California.

Sapodilla

The sapodilla, or naseberry, is a native of Central America and the Yucatan Peninsula in Mexico. The Maya Indians, and other Indians living before them, tapped the sapodilla tree for its white sap, called chicle. This sap, when boiled, sweetened, and flavored, becomes chewing gum.

The sapodilla — or chicle tree, as it is sometimes called — has handsome, shiny, dark-green leaves, and grows to a height of about 60 feet. The fruit is apple-shaped, with a skin that is rusty-brown in color and often rough in texture. The sweet inside pulp — the part that is eaten — is yellowish or orange, and is honey-flavored. Sapodillas have from one to several glossy brown or black seeds.

55

Sapote

Sapote

The sapote is a member of the Sapodilla family. Visitors to marketplaces in Guatemala may pass by rows of sapotes, thinking they are baked potatoes, for this is what some of them look like. But inside this strange-appearing fruit is a delicious reddish-orange pulp and a single shiny black seed. This seed is often used for flavoring purposes because it has the scent and flavor of bitter almonds. The sapote is a native of Central America.

56

Cherimoya

Cherimoya

The large Custard Apple family includes tropical trees that produce the cherimoya, the pond apple, the soursop, the sweetsop, and the custard apple itself. Cherimoyas are native to the valleys of the Andes Mountains in Peru, and were a favorite dessert of the Inca Indians. In fact, the name "cherimoya" came from a word in Quechua, the language of the Incas. The egg-shaped or heart-shaped fruit grows on a medium-sized tree about 25 feet tall. The fruit may weigh anywhere from one to fifteen pounds. Its skin is made up of green overlapping scales. The flesh inside is white and is a little bit like custard. Cherimoyas are occasionally grown in the southern parts of Florida and California.

Soursop

Soursop

The fast-growing soursop tree reaches a height of 25 feet and produces large, rough fruits, deep green in color. These fruits may weigh from eight to ten pounds. Their white flesh is juicy and tart. Natives of the tropics strain the soursop's pulp through a sieve to make a drink somewhat like lemonade, or freeze the juice into a sherbert.

Custard Apple

This fruit is grown in Mexico, the northern parts of South America, southern Florida, and on many Caribbean islands. The fruit is heart-shaped and contains a creamy flesh and many large brown seeds. When custard apples are chilled, the flesh resembles ice cream and is eaten with a spoon.

Mangosteen

The mangosteen is a native of the Malay Peninsula. Today it is grown in India, Ceylon, and the East and West Indies. The shiny-leaved mangosteen trees are small and bear a fruit that is a berry about the size and shape of a tangerine, but is dark red to purplish-brown in color. The inside flesh is snowy-white and juicy. It is arranged in sections — five to seven of them — held in a pinkish-violet cup. This tasty center contains brown seeds which may be cooked and eaten. In 1770, Captain James Cook, a famous English navigator, ate mangosteens on the island of Java and thought that "nothing can be more delicious."

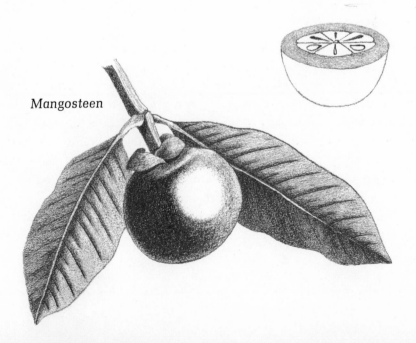

Mangosteen

Akee

Akee

The akee is a native of tropical Africa and is now found also in the West Indies. It was probably brought there many years ago by African slaves. The curious fruits are borne in clusters on a smallish tree with beautiful foliage. They are about the size of lemons. They turn brilliant red when ripe, then split lengthwise into three parts, showing three large black seeds which stick out of a white mass of edible pulp. This pulp resembles brains and in the Spanish-speaking parts of the West Indies is often called by a name that means "vegetable brain." When the pulp is stewed, or fried in butter, it makes a tasty vegetable. It may also be eaten raw.

The akee is a dangerous fruit. When it is not ripe or when it is overripe, it is poisonous. In fact, the seeds and purplish flesh near them are also poisonous.

Litchi Nut

The Chinese litchi nut is not really a nut, but a fruit. It is a native of southern China, where it has grown for thousands of years. Litchis have a thin, papery shell that is warty. On the tree, the fruits are bright red. They measure about one inch in diameter and grow in loose clusters — about twenty fruits to a cluster. The inside flesh is whitish, and tastes somewhat like Tokay grapes. When dried, this flesh becomes dark brown and has a sweet-acid flavor. The Chinese sections of many American cities have shops where imported dried litchi nuts are sold, as this fruit is a favorite with people from the Orient.

Litchi nut

INDEX